Art to the Glory of God

Art to the Glory of God

John Barber

WIPF & STOCK · Eugene, Oregon

ART TO THE GLORY OF GOD

Wipf & Stock
An Imprint of Wipf and Stock Publishers
199 W. 8th Ave., Suite 3
Eugene, OR 97401
www.wipfandstock.com

ISBN 13: 978-1-60899-310-9

Manufactured in the U.S.A.

To Paul, my son and aspiring painter

Contents

Foreword

THIS SHORT introduction to the issue of God and art reminds me first of the question I was asked some time ago, "Chris, can you paint God?" I responded by saying, "No." But I followed up with the observation that I could paint aspects of the attributes of God. The Christian artist is often struggling without guidance for we have a very long Protestant tradition of anti-visual art. The search for an honest look at art from a theological point of view has been taken up by several scholars, theologians, as well as by Christian artists, and much has been written on that subject in the last four decades. This booklet is a good addition to this dialogue that is now taking place between artists and the Church. We can all learn from each other and need to begin to appreciate that there are many ways in which to glorify God.

This booklet is written for the Church, for theological students, and for art students. It is my hope that especially theological students will benefit from a better understanding of the role of art within a biblical framework. It may come as a surprise to you that the first person who was inspired by God to make a worship environment was not a prophet, nor a priest, nor a king, but an artist. In the book of Exodus, chapter 31, we are introduced to Bezalel, whom the Lord called and inspired to build the tabernacle and all the items in and around the holy tent of God. Bezalel enhanced the worship experience according to God's plan, from tent to altar, from vestments to vessels. God took this whole business of the worship space rather seriously.

John Barber challenges the role and task of art within the Christian community. Great art is missing from the places of worship. Why? That is the question that is explored in the beginning and followed by an introduction to other measuring criteria. Some of these will invite further discussion, and that is good. There are three sections on color that are especially interesting: Color's Appeal, God and His World of Color, and the Color of Revelation. Like the author, I hope that this booklet will continue the dialogue about art and how we can best glorify the Lord together.

Chris Overvoorde
Professor Emeritus,
Department of Art and Art History
Calvin College

Introduction

Years ago, I was privileged to be a student at the Yale University Institute of Sacred Music. The Institute is an interdisciplinary think-tank that is shared by the Yale Divinity School and the Yale Graduate School of Music. I attended classes in both schools. The principle focus of the Institute is to further study and dialogue on the relationship of Christianity and culture. My role at the Institute also permitted me to take courses at the Department of Christianity and the Arts, where I studied art history (principally painting and architecture) and many of the underlying religious themes found in numerous art masterpieces. During my few years at the Institute, I arrived at many conclusions regarding the relationship between Christianity and culture—all of which have since matured.

One result of my deliberations over this mutual relationship is a book that I wrote titled *The Road From Eden: Studies in Christianity and Culture*. The book has a great deal to say about many areas of society and culture, art and art history in particular. Though my formal training is in the area of music, I learned many years ago that the best place to discern the imprint of Christianity upon the forms of Western culture is found in the medium of art—painting and architecture, specifically. Frankly, the history of culture is embodied in the history of art. As I have stated many times before, the student that knows little of art history knows little of cultural history.

An unexpected byproduct of *The Road from Eden* was a desire on my part to think more critically about what makes art great. Knowledge of art history is one thing. But knowledge of how one goes about creating a masterpiece is quite another. Truth be told, I can't paint or sculpt; even my stick-figures leave something to be desired. Nonetheless, there came a point in my study of Christianity's contribution to the contrasts, currents, and trends in Western culture that caused me to pause and self-reflect, "Wait a minute. What is it about all of these magnificent creations of art that sets them on a higher plane from lesser examples?" So, my interest in *what* happened in art history shifted to *how* art becomes great—the mechanics of art. This is a difficult question, certainly because there are so many different examples from art history to examine. The criteria for what makes a composition "great" has changed from epoch to epoch. But are there not some common ingredients that make great art, great?

Added to my continuing interest is a deeper question. I am a Christian. Consequently, I am ever-mindful of the fact that all that is done on this earthly globe is done before a watching God who appraises all the works of our hands. So, for this writer, the question of great art is inextricably woven into the question of how one does art that glorifies God. Now, it is possible to create something that glorifies God but, according to the critic's eye, is poorly done. On the other hand, it is feasible to create a piece of art that stands the test of time, but which glorifies man. My purpose in this brief work is to seek a synthesis of the two ideas: to offer some suggestions on how the artist can do great art that glorifies God. Beneath all of this is my enduring quest to see the Christian community become, once more, the source of magnificent, world-shaping art.

It is my earnest hope that the artist reading this booklet, whether an apprentice, or advanced, will find within its pages a true source of encouragement and some insights that can improve his craft.

John Barber, PhD
2010

Art to the Glory of God

CONTEMPORARY TRENDS in modern art have certainly become a hot button issue. From Andres Serrano's blasphemous *Piss Christ*, a large photo of a crucifix immersed in urine, to Chris Ofili's controversial depiction of the Virgin Mary with elephant dung, to Renee Cox's *Yo Mama's Last Supper*, a five-panel photo which depicts Christ as a nude woman, there are ample reasons for Christians to be concerned about the growing irreverence in art. Moreover, both Serrano and Ofili received financial support from the United States Government (National Endowment for the Arts or NEA), a move that incensed cultural conservatives and which motivated them to put pressure on their elected officials to eliminate government funding for the NEA. We have also heard of the publicly funded art exhibition at the Gallery of Modern Art in Glasgow, Scotland where many visitors wrote blasphemous comments and obscenities across the pages of a displayed copy of the Bible. The exhibit also includes a video of a woman tearing pages from the Bible and stuffing them into her bra, knickers, and mouth.

While it is tempting to follow other writers who have detailed many examples of sacrilegious art and suggest ways in which the Church can fight to eliminate them, I have chosen to take a different direction. The reason is because the above discussion, although it is important, is not about art. It is a debate over morality. As we shall soon see, ethical and moral considerations function as non-negotiable ingredients in the creation of art. Nevertheless, art must not be limited to these factors.

I dare say that most believers would have little to say about art were it not for the fact that much of it has become scandalous.

But the future of art will continue to be in question if Christians remain little more than art critics. Art also calls for our *positive* contribution—something that requires much study and thoughtful reflection. However, the Church of today is not doing enough to offer serious reflection upon the nature of art and its role within the Christian community. The Church is producing no great artists in the line of Rembrandt, Van Gogh, or Rouault (at least none that have risen to prominence). The word "masterpiece" is missing from the vocabulary of the Church. But what is more disappointing is the reason for this failure. The Church no longer encourages great art.

The flourishing, artistic environment and the pressure to produce top-quality compositions that once gave us Michelangelo's ceiling of the Sistine Chapel, or Giotto's priceless fresco, *The Life of St. Francis*, has vanished. And, with rare exception, so has the wealth of gifted artisans that once marked the Church as the leader in the creation of magnificent works of art. But is not this failure to encourage the finest of artistic compositions the result of another more significant failure—that the Church no longer encourages great culture? *Today the scandal is not the existence of outrageous art. Rather, the greater scandal is that the Church has no great art to offer in its place.*

Nonetheless, this is not a new problem. It began when, after the sixteenth-century reformation of the Church, there emerged a needed and renewed zeal for the law of God. True, many blessings came to the Church as a result of its newfound commitment to the Law. However, the unfortunate by-product of people's enthusiasm for the second commandment in particular ("Thou shalt not make for thyself an idol, or any likeness of what is in heaven above or on earth beneath or in the waters under the earth"), was an unnecessary, institutional suspicion of *all* art, which has lasted in many quarters to this day.

I would be wrong to suggest that the Church's anxiety over art is purely the result of a misreading of the second commandment.

The influence of Christian pietism in the creation of a Christian sub-culture affords an equally important explanation for the widespread scarcity of great art within the Church. Pietism has become a modern day Harold Hill, who once warned River City of the dangers of a "pool-hall, libertine men, and scarlet women," but who today warns the world of the dangers of painting, film, poetry, literature, and music.

In 1981, Franky Schaeffer, in his book, *Addicted to Mediocrity: 20th Century Christians and the Arts*, commented that the Church had abdicated its role in the creation of great art, and instead followed, rather than led, popular culture with the production of "Christian doodads, trinkets, tee-shirts, and bumper stickers."[1]

Sadly, years later, little has changed. Most art that is either appropriated by the Church or is produced by believers continues to be mediocre. Christian clip-art has become a metaphor for contemporary Christian art, which reveals a type of pseudo-intellectualism, or sweet Jesus mentality, that fails to provide a vision of real beauty and, therefore, of transcendence. What is the answer?

1. Schaeffer, *Addicted to Mediocrity,* back cover.

A Modern-Day Renaissance

We must seek to birth a reformation of the fine arts within the Church. We must seek to encourage what the twentieth-century, French priest and artist, Marie Alain Couturier, sought to encourage—great art, sacred art. Problematically, the Church's disdain for indecent art, and what it believes should be a proper moral and political response to it, has become its position on art. If believers are going to demonstrate obedience to the cultural mandate, we must balance our fight against lewd art with seeking to advance great art. The following points are intended to help the Church rediscover the nature of great art, to the glory of our King, so that it might begin to produce it once again. Most of my remarks will center on painting because, within the fine arts, it is the easiest to use as a forum for discussing our topic. However, most of the conclusions we arrive at regarding painting can be applied to all other areas within the fine arts with only minor modification.

For art to be great, the artist must have a saving relationship with God. This point represents Christianity's distinctive contribution to the furtherance of great art. As I previously mentioned, there is a moral component to art. More precisely, the act of doing art takes place within a moral context. Art is simply a creative extension of an artist's spiritual values and worldview, which help to define his relationship to God. Every brush stroke, film edit, musical phrase, or architectural design must therefore exhibit the quality of *aesthetic deference* to the Lord of all creativity.

The Dutch theologian, Cornelius Van Til, argued there is no such thing as a "brute fact"—a part of reality that somehow escapes Divine interpretation. Likewise, there is no such thing as brute art. All forms of art, as they articulate a moral position, summon Holy judgment. The ancient prophet Isaiah declared that the acceptability of man's work before God cannot be divorced from the matter of ethics: "And all our righteousness are as filthy rags" (Isa 64:6, NIV). Without a redemptive relationship between the artist and his Creator, the artist's labor, although it may reflect the interests of beauty in a broad sense, will fall short in gaining God's full approval. It is therefore not enough to seek great art in beautiful colors, sounds, proportions, and shapes. Rather, *right values* must also flow from the artist's hands, as those values flow from his heart.

It was another gifted Dutch theologian, Hans Rookmaaker, who said the main reason for the decline of modern art is the fact that man's creativity is marked by his infectious desire for human autonomy from God's ethical demands.[2] Rookmaaker saw the history of art in terms of man's struggle to define both himself and his world ontologically and epistemologically. "Who am I?" "What is there to know?" These questions, according to Rookmaaker, have fueled man's search for meaning, which in turn, have given rise to his conscious creativity in the arts.

Unfortunately, man's historic search for meaning has not always been marked by his quest for the One, true God of the Bible. Instead, the spiritual search of many artists has been characterized by arrogant rebellion against the Lord. The only hope for modern man, and consequently for his art, is to return to God. Where art is broken, it is because man is broken by sin. Art is nothing more than an image of something that exists in God's universe. But man is also an image—the image of God. If man, as the image of God, remains broken and is not restored in Christ, how can his broken image produce a complete and meaningful image of something else?

This begs an important question: Does this mean that only Christians are capable of great art? For example, Pablo Picasso was not a believer, yet he is considered one of the greatest paint-

2. Rookmaaker, *Modern Art and the Death of Culture.*

ers of all time. Undoubtedly, Picasso, and other gifted unbelievers like him, demonstrated technical brilliance and aesthetic vision in their compositions. But what is important to remember is that these artists were working from a *deficit*. While from a human perspective, their life-production may be considered great, sin had reduced them to mere vestiges of the image of God, meaning that their work never reached its *full* potential. In a *spiritual* sense, their work was *not* sound. Indeed, had Picasso trusted Christ and been restored in the image of the Creator-God, his genius would have been even greater! Another Dutch churchman, Klaas Schilder, in commenting upon the spiritual deficit in unbelieving artists, remarked, "Our conclusion then is that culture is never more than a mere attempt and that, since it is restricted to remnants only, it is a matter of tragedy. God has indeed left something behind in fallen man. But these are only 'small remnants' of his original gifts...they can never produce any work that is sound."[3]

One might argue that since it is common, the world over, to refer to the traditions, symbols, and habits of a people-group as culture that even the unregenerate can create the best, possible art. But to argue this way is to over-generalize what is good and great in God's eyes. In Gen 2:15, God instructs Adam to cultivate the Garden of Eden. Culture is of course the natural result of man's cultivation of the earth's natural resources. Thus, from a *quantitative* viewpoint, "to cultivate" is a creation mandate and is thus the work of all men formed in the image of God. However, the original context of Gen 2:15 limits "cultivate," in *qualitative* terms, to an intensely God-centered activity. The qualitative nature of man's pursuit of culture is laid out previously in Gen 1:31. "God saw all that He had made, and behold, it was very good." The creation is "very good" because it was made by a very good God. Thus, art cannot be interpreted apart from the ethical concerns of the Creator—how God defines "very good."

3. Schilder, *Christ and Culture*, 59.

Great art is what is done out of covenant faithfulness to God. Leon G. Wencelius remarked, "Culture is the fulfillment of purposive molding of nature in execution of the creative will of God."[4] Granted, God's curse upon the earth, in response to man's rebellion in the Garden, has affected its unspoiled quality. Yet, Paul can still encourage us to receive all things with thanksgiving on the basis that "everything God created is good" (2 Tim 4:4, KJV). Moreover, God's unchanging goodness, as revealed in Scripture, still functions as the ultimate, ethical standard for man's artistic labor.

Although sin has rendered man dead in sins, Christ is the restorer of man. Indeed, God's purpose for the world is to restore everything that was lost at the Fall—both in man and in the rest of creation—to its proper role of worshipping and glorifying Him. In Christ, man receives back those elements of the image of God that were lost through sin, and his life and work are redirected to the glory of God. Only Christ can restore art, because only Christ can restore the artist's heart so that his full potential to create can be fully realized.

Great art that glorifies God is the result of an artist who understands his role in furthering his craft. The artist's role includes a practical level that is concerned with *artistic validity*. He must ask, "*Why* am I doing this?" "Do I create for the love of art or for the love of money?" "Do I work tirelessly to churn out productions just to be accepted by the local critics, or is my work intended as an offering to God?" If an artist's motivations are not in keeping with the nature of great art, he will not create it.

Additionally, the artist's role includes a purely creative level that focuses on the *goal of artistic expression*. An artist must ask, "*What* am I doing?" "Do I have a goal for my composition?" This is an important question because the Bible teaches that God is goal-oriented. A simple reading of the Bible, from Genesis to Revelation, proves that God is leading history to a glorious point. While explicating the fundamentals of a biblical worldview before

4. Wencelius, "The Word of God and Culture," 160.

students, I like to highlight the God-driven, eschatological tilt of history with this remark: "The world and all that it contains is subject to the eternal purpose and plan of God." Clearly, God has a goal for art—an eternal goal. Art is to serve the forward movement of history toward its climactic end when then all things, including art, will be subjected to Christ (see 1 Cor 15:27). How can art serve this noble end? Art facilitates God's plan when it *glorifies* Him. But how can an artist glorify God through a painting, for example?

What the Artist Is Not

To BEGIN with, a painter (and artists generally) must understand his limits. He is not a revelator. The inspiration he receives is unlike that received by holy men of old, who spoke, "Thus says the Lord." His is not the job of special revelation, but of *general* revelation. Like the image of God in man and the wonders of tree, hill, and sky, the beauty of art directs our attention to the fundamental truths of the existence of God and of His Divine attributes. This is as far as an artist can take us. Although, through his use of brush and palette, a painter can *represent* the meaning of God's special work in Christ, he cannot *impart* its meaning. This work is reserved for the Word of God in cooperation with the Holy Spirit.

Thus, the artist is not a prophet, but he is *almost* a prophet. While the artist shares the prophet's role in confronting us with the fundamental issues of life, the prophet differs in his ability to resolve these issues with unmistakable clarity.

The artist is not a priest, but he is *almost* a priest. Although his canvas is a world full of symbols that represent a spiritual reality beyond themselves, the priest takes us beyond what symbols *can* mean to what they *do* mean.

Poised Between Two Realms

IF THE above descriptions fall short of describing the artist's goal, what can illustrate his goal more fully? The goal of the artist is to be like the *horizon*—touching both finite world and infinite heaven. Suspended as it were between two realms, the artist's job is to link the material world of paint and canvas (or possibly sheet music, celluloid, or words), with the supernatural world of transcendent values. In Van Gogh's *Night Café*, the painter, and former missionary, uses color as language. He paints what he sees with his soul and uses color to exaggerate his message. By moving from a dark foreground to a light background, we are drawn backwards into the painting. The painting wants to draw us from our world of the common and the ordinary to a world of transcendent quality, objective meaning, and thus, the God of all meaning.

At the same time, however, an artist must not permit a deliberate goal to shackle pure, unencumbered self-expression. The life of great art is born out of the unhampered spirit within the artist, working with a diligent hand in light of the respect, humility, and modesty he brings to his subject. M.A. Couturier expressed it best: "A work is truly a work of art only if it comes out of the depths of its author's spirit, and from even further down than that—I would say out of his guts."[1]

A man once asked me, "John, do you establish a goal before you preach and know exactly where you are going in a message, or do you follow some loosely prepared notes and allow for the inspiration of the Holy Spirit?" I replied, "I think through every word before preaching, and then when I begin, I forget it." Likewise, a painter, for example, must have a goal before taking up the brush. Then he must forget it. He must organize at every level. But once he begins to

1. "Religious Consciousness," class notes.

paint he must put all of it aside and permit his gift to take flight. An artist who leads his work too closely will cause it to be cramped and stifled. The gift must lead, or else the art will suffer.

Practically speaking, what must an artist accomplish in order for his composition to glorify God? Let's answer this question as though we were observing a painting.

Practical Steps Toward a Masterpiece

For a painting to glorify God, the composition must, from the outset, direct my sensory interest to the work itself. Beyond this, I should be able to understand that the artist has worked the physical materials in such a way that I sense the joy, serenity, or horror he felt while painting. Additionally, I should discern a Christian *consciousness* in the composition through the artist's use of color and form. And I should sense his faith reaction to specific social and historical forces leading to the consummation of all things—the "eschatological tilt" of history mentioned earlier.

But the artist must go further. Not only must he impress me with his journey of faith, but also he must *arouse* my faith. His creation must contain the power of inner suggestion, the power to inspire. An artist's goal must be to provide people *a point of departure* to a deeper reality that transcends the finite and the mundane. He should provide a vision of God that stirs within us a sense of holy awe and wonder. Through his work he should seek to usher us into the presence of a world of absolute meaning through his use of less than absolute lines, forms, and shapes. And he should strive to inspire all of our senses with a vision of beauty that would otherwise remain inaccessible to us were it not for the presence of his work.

Through Rouault's *The Holy Countenance*, the painter wants to stimulate reflection on Christ. Using luminous colors, simplicity of form, and solemnity of contour, Rouault conceives Christ in pain and suffering due to the effects of sin in the world. Christ came to bear the sins of many and to identify with our suffering. Yet comfort is fleeting. Rouault also wants to confront us in our disbelief. It's as if the painting declares, "You decide!" Rouault's

Christ is, as the artist Cognac put it, "The way of grace between man's misery and the love of God." It was the misery and loneliness of man that was Rouault's personal and Christian starting point.

To capture a message with this level of impact in a composition, an artist must also be a *visionary*. He must consider his materials and their use only in light of the general effect of the whole. Yet he cannot know whether he is achieving this effect, except for his vision for the work. Additionally, an artist must foresee that his composition will be made of *little compositions*, which may at first appear antagonistic to each other but which, once put together, will serve to clarify the meaning of the whole. The Russian Orthodox painter, Wassily Kandinsky, said, "The creation of the various forms, which, by standing in different relationships to each other, decide the composition of the whole."[1]

Now let's look at a closely related point that enables an artist to create great art and glorify God in his work.

Great art is that which embodies great content. What accounts for the tragedy in Massaccio's *The Expulsion from Paradise*, the power of Bach's *Mass in B minor,* the grief of Rembrandt's *Descent from the Cross*, or the soul of T. S. Eliot's poetry? It is content. But what is content? Content is more than what we see or hear. It is other than paint, form, line, notes, sound, words, juxtaposition of elements, or artistic convention. It goes deeper. Rather, content is the *total* effect of a work of art, something the individual parts of the work cannot account for. Content is that which transcends the material elements of a work and which continues to draw us to it, to dwell on it and be pulled into it. Content is the *life* of the work.

All artists know they must achieve content, but virtually no one can produce a map to get there. Rather, content is that which is *sought*. Thus, the contemporary painter, Joel C. Sheesley, looks to the writer of Hebrews to say that art content is "The substance of things hoped for."[2] I agree that art content is difficult to achieve.

1. Ibid.
2. Sheesley, "Content."

Nevertheless, there are procedural factors one can consider in order to facilitate content in a work.

Let's look at just three elements of art content: space, color, and form. We begin with a consideration of space in the art of architectural design.

The God That Is There and Not There

IS THERE more space in the Louisiana Superdome or in a chapel? Now let's be clear. I'm not asking which one has more room, but rather which one has more "space." If the architect has captured content in his design, then the answer is the chapel has more space. The explanation is that the chapel contains the *presence of absence*. Standing in the chapel, you sense something is missing. It is not that there is something that needs to be added to the room in order to complete it, rather, there is something present in the room that is greater than the room. This "something" is also somewhere else. And it draws you to where it is.

Jesus personified the presence of absence. He was fully God and fully man. He was divine and human. His divinity pointed a way to God, while His humanity pointed to us. Theologians call it the "mystery of the incarnation." However, we must be careful not to allow our experience of the Christian mystery to become an exercise in abstraction. Christ is Emmanuel—God with us. Our experience of Christ is grounded upon God's self-revelation in history. Otherwise, faith becomes thoughtless and unthinking. It produces faithlessness. In all, it is the mystery of Christ which creates within us a sense of reverence and holy wonder and which draws us to Him. Now let's return to the chapel.

What makes a room a chapel? It is the presence of absence—the mystery. In the foothills of the Vosges Mountains of France is the chapel at Ronchamp, designed by Le Corbusier. Within the chapel, *light* is the key to creating a sense of mystery. The unpretentious use of colored glass makes the space neither too bright nor dull. The building allows in only *prayerful* light through the use of blues, soft yellows, and whites. The peaceful atmosphere with no distracting elements makes the space come alive. The building is neither didactic nor entertaining, but powerful. It displays this power through simple use of perfect lines and forms. However, the lines and forms are not perfect in a stylized sense, but rather are perfect as perfection is found in nature. Through modest use of materials, we learn that less is more. We are inspired, not manipulated.

In addition to communicating spiritual power, the chapel also conveys architectural *action*. It is not cut *into* nature, but seems to flow *out of* nature on its way toward heaven. There is also an architectural *language* to the chapel, an acoustical phenomenon, which allows it to speak. The aesthetic effect of the whole creates a depth dimension that takes us beyond appearances. The content of the chapel is experienced in everything from the artistry of the pews, to the innovative use of a crabshell roof, to the eloquence of the rain barrels. The presence of absence can also be achieved in other spheres of art, including music, painting, sculpture, and film.

The chapel reminds us of a point that I made earlier: that we, as a body of believers, have generally failed to adopt a set of positive cultural values toward great art. Of course, here I am thinking especially about the architectural spaces we have set apart for corporate worship. Such places have, on the whole, remained provincial. Many of our church edifices are heralded, not for their architectural action and language, but for the fact that they are "multi-purpose." But ought not people who claim theological integrity in their shared devotion and cultural consciousness seek to embody such integrity in the spaces they use for worship and prayer? We are living in a day when attempts at Christian cultural reform are almost entirely limited to the arena of electoral politics. Let us not forget; however, that cultural reform and transformation is also measured by the quality of the witness churches present to the world through the language of art and architecture.

A key element used in art is the use of color. As we continue our look at art content, let's focus on how color is used in the medium of painting.

Only a Biblical Worldview Accounts for Color's Appeal

THE LAST of the great artists of the Renaissance and the first of the modern era, Eugène Delacroix, observed, "Everyone knows that yellow, orange, and red suggest ideas of joy and plenty."[1] We would all agree that color bears the power to suggest. We would also agree that the language of color is universal. Red has the same effect upon a Frenchman as it does upon an American.

There is another universally accepted notion. Bright colors are complimented by sharp forms (e.g. a yellow triangle), and soft colors are well suited by round forms (e.g. a blue circle). This example further illustrates the universal language of color. But it also demonstrates there is a pattern to color in its relationship to other elements in painting. Indeed, if we were to introduce considerations such as texture, contour, harmony, and contrast, we would see that, depending on how we use color in light of these factors, color's effect upon men would continue to follow a given pattern. But how do we account for the universal language of color?

The answer is found in God. Specifically, it is discovered in God's unity and simplicity. It is the unity and simplicity of the Godhead that supplies the ontological backdrop for our interpretation of color. Yes, there is a subjective element in our interpretation of color. But this fact only further illustrates that for color to elicit a given, universal response it must be part of a greater fabric—a world of relationships that find their meaning in God. In what way can an artist use color to give glory to God?

He can use the *function* of color to express spiritual truth. It was Kandinsky who recognized that color falls into two great

1. Delacroix, *D Eugene Delacroix*.

divisions: warm and cold, light and dark. Therefore, he taught that color has four shades of appeal: warm and light or warm and dark, or cold and light or cold and dark. "Generally speaking, warmth or cold in a color means an approach respectively to yellow or blue . . . The movement is a horizontal one, the warm colors approaching the spectator, the cold ones retreating from him."[2]

Kandinsky also taught that color functions according to an excentric or concentric movement. "If two circles are drawn and painted respectively yellow and blue, brief concentration will reveal in the yellow a spreading movement out from the center, and a noticeable approach to the spectator. The blue, on the other hand, moves in upon itself, like a snail retreating into its shell, and draws away from the spectator."[3] Based upon Kandinsky's insights, let's see how God—the Master Artist—uses the function of color to convey spiritual truth.

2. Kandinsky, *Concerning the Spiritual in Art*, 36.

3. Ibid., 36–37.

God and His World of Color

ALTHOUGH GOD painted the sun using a variety of colors, it would appear to us as excentric yellow (or white, if we could gaze directly into it). Thus, the sun's color is in harmony with its function: radiating outward and communicating warmth. This fact points to a spiritual truth. As yellow radiates outward, serving to communicate the sun's radiance and warmth, so also the Son is the "radiance of His glory" (Heb 1:3), who came into the world to communicate the Father's warmth. Also, like the reaching of the sun's rays, I did not reach out to God, but He reached out to me.

Then there is the relationship between the *blue* of the sky and the *green* of the earth. Typically, blue is a heavenly color. It creates a feeling of eternal rest. Its concentric movement causes it to pull in and away from the observer. Also, there is the concentric green of the earth. Green is the most restful of all colors. However, green differs from blue in that it does not convey supernatural rest, but earthly peace. Furthermore, green is the result of combining yellow with blue. Likewise, the redemption of the earth (green) is the product of the work of the Son (yellow) who, in heaven's economy (blue), came to seek and to save those who are lost. Also, because green is the product of the excentric movement of yellow and the concentric movement of blue, the effect on the eye is therefore neutral, motionless. Similarly, by stilling the storm, Jesus illustrated His power to save and that the earth's response to the salvation of God is to be still.

The Color of Revelation

THE BIBLE is also replete with God's masterful use of color. The four horsemen of the Apocalypse (Rev 6:1–8) appear in colors of *white, red, black, and ashen*. The first horse is "white," and he rides out to conquer. White is the most reaching of all colors. Because white is the absence of color, it is full of possibilities. No wonder it is associated in Scripture with holiness, the Holy Spirit, and the glory of God. On the other hand, white is difficult to make warm. Like the earth's poles, it wants to be cold, old, and impenetrable. White can therefore have a negative effect upon our lives. A perfect complement for one that goes out to conquer.

The second horse is "red," and brings war to the earth. This is the color of power and intensity. Kandinsky sees red as neither excentric, nor concentric. It is "motion within itself."[1] Red conveys the feeling of strength and determination. It is fitting, then, that this horse comes to withdraw the Spirit of God and take peace from the earth that men might slay each other. Red, of course, is also the color of blood.

The third horse is "black" and brings famine to the earth. Black is not the color of death, but the color of the motionlessness and nothingness that precedes death. Used as a background in painting, black causes other colors to stand forward and become sharp. Likewise, it shall be in the moments before death, in this case brought by world famine, that the important issues of life stand out and become clear.

The fourth horse is "ashen." This is the color of death. Ashen is a derivative of gray, which is produced by blending black and white—colors that stand at opposite ends of the color spectrum.

1. Ibid., Figure II, 36–37.

Jesus said, "I am the alpha and the omega, the beginning and the end" (Rev 21:6). Just as a combination of black and white produces the pale effect of ashen, so also it is Christ alone who has the authority (see Rev 6:8) to produce this rider's dread effects.

Now we move from color to the final content element of art. Let's take a look at the meaning of form, again through the medium of painting.

The Shape of Great Art

THE STUDY of form in painting is a study of culture and its values. Before the advent of modern art, artists paid much more attention to the use of form than perhaps any other element. For example, Renaissance artists such as Giovanni Bellini, Leonardo da Vinci, and Jan Van Eyck endeavored to create *absolute form* in their compositions. They did so out of a deep and persistent attitude reflected throughout the Middle Ages that the intellect can obtain knowledge of God only insofar as corporeal objects are related to God and reveal Him. Remember, most people didn't have Bibles at that time. There was therefore a much greater emphasis placed upon natural theology and the need for the physical world to provide *all* knowledge of God. Michelangelo was perhaps the greatest painter and sculptor who ever lived. He was so consumed with his pursuit for the perfect form that he was driven nearly mad.

It is with Goya (1746–1828) and Delacroix (1798–1863) that painting takes its first step toward modern art. A less rigid appraisal of form now becomes accepted in favor of using the imagination. Idealized landscapes begin to be painted by Constable, Turner, Corot, and Courbet. However, it is with the advent of Cubism, and artists Pablo Picasso (1881–1973) and Georges Braque (1882–1963), that the cultural and theological ideals of Renaissance high art, and their impact on form, begin to quickly unravel. The cubist style rejected the traditional techniques of creating form and instead emphasized the flat, two-dimensional surface of the picture plane. All the time-honored, artistic and cultural theories that assisted artists in their attempt to capture spiritual meaning in material objects were discarded. Instead, cubists sought the creation of a "new reality." The total breakdown of cultural ideals in art came with the birth of Dada. Marcel Duchamp (1887–1968) was its leading figure. A product of the philosophy of nihilism, Dada was a mostly western European movement that sought to destroy traditional culture and aesthetic forms in favor of surrealism and "authentic reality."

My brief sketch of art history is intended to make a point: a crisis in artistic form results from a crisis in cultural norms. But the Christian artist must not reflect the low standards of a culture; he is called to elevate them.

How can a Christian use form in art to glorify God and help reverse culture's headlong dive into meaninglessness? Here are three general guidelines.

Art form should be understandable. Considered by many to be the greatest art masterpiece of the twentieth century, Picasso's *Guernica* was painted in memory of the bombing of Guernica, France by the Germans during World War II. The problem is that absolutely no one knows what it means. And Picasso refused to offer an explanation for his composition. This approach to art form is unacceptable for a Christian. Paul writes, "But thanks be to God, who always leads us in His triumph in Christ, and manifests through us the sweet aroma of the knowledge of Him in every place" (1 Cor 2:16). God wants the believer to manifest the fragrance of his knowledge of Christ in everything he does, including his art. Art form should not veil one's knowledge of Christ behind a curtain of abstractions and inner meanings. Instead, every part of one's composition should bear the unmistakable aroma of Christ by reflecting the beauty and truth that belongs to Him.

Art form should be redemptive. The Norwegian painter, Edward Munch (1863–1944) is considered the father of Expressionism—a vague term that describes many works of art created during the twentieth century that are charged with emotion. Munch's most recognized composition is *The Scream*. Through the use of intense colors and ghost-like forms, the artist captures what he believes to be man's greatest fear—the fear of living.

Fear is unquestionably a common theme found in Scripture. For example, the Bible says, "The fear of the Lord is the beginning of knowledge" (Prov 1:7). What stands out to me in this well-known verse of Scripture is that holy fear is not a dead-end road, but the beginning of something great—the knowledge of God. Munch, on the other hand, represents a trend in art that not only rejected the possibility of knowing God, but also resigned itself to the abyss of despair. While Christian art is free to affirm the plight of humankind and man's age-old struggle with the meaning of existence, it must also depict the way out of this struggle. It must capture the way of grace and redemption that leads people out of the hollowness and terror of facing the future without hope. The Bible says, "For God hath not given us the spirit of fear; but of power, and of love, and of a sound mind" (2 Tim 1:7, KJV).

Art form should balance subjective feeling with objective truth. In direct opposition to the extreme subjectivism of Dada, is the French artist, Piet Mondrian (1872–1944). He is known for being the first painter to reject all subjective feeling in art. His work represented what is called, Neo-plasticism. The goal of art form, according to Mondrian, is to avoid any personal involvement with one's subject. Focusing inward involves participation, and participation with objects introduces human suffering and death. If you permit your emotions to follow nature, Mondrian wrote in 1920, you have to accept "whatever is capricious and twisted in nature." Mondrian even refused to attach imaginative titles to his compositions for fear that he might prejudice the *objective* message of his work (e.g. *Ocean 5; Composition with Red, Yellow, and Blue*).

Although today's culture may be guilty of wallowing in subjectivism, the Christian artist must be free to enlist his feelings, personal experiences, and sanctified imagination in the creation of a composition. The Christian artist is a unique individual. God has given to him the ability to do something which no other person can do in his place: be himself. His work must therefore demonstrate that he is "fearfully and wonderfully made" (Ps 139:14). An artist must study great art in order to do great art. He may even want to copy other great artists' use of form in order to learn technique. But ultimately what separates one great artist from another is an artist's *personality*.

On the other hand, we must also be *met* by truth in art. This is the objective element. An art masterpiece expresses not only an artist's inner-self and causes the observer to ask, "What does this mean to me?", it also confronts people with the "wholly other." A composition that lacks a transcendent quality—that fails to challenge people with the immeasurable truth of God—fails the test of truly great art. Schelling said, "Beauty is the infinite presented in the finite."[2]

Emile Nolde (1867–1956) was a Christian German expressionist who devoted himself to capturing Christian themes in mostly woodcuts, drawings, and watercolors. "One of the founders of Die Brücke (the Bridge) in 1905 along with Erich Heckel, Ernst Ludwig Kirschner, and Karl Schmidt-Rottluff," Nolde sought to use his compositions to strike a prophetic chord and awaken Germany to a "new, free, passionate age." The Nazi's condemned Nolde's work as "degenerate." [3] Nolde's most famous print, *The Prophet,* is a case study in how to balance raw subjective emotion with the light of objective truth in art.

2. Schelling, "On Earth."
3. Spaightwood Galleries, "Emile Nolde."

Final Thoughts

My hope is that this brief work has offered guidance to the Church in its effort to produce great works of art that glorify the Creator of all. Perhaps the reader uses a different set of standards to judge and/or create great art. That you agree with my particular set of criteria is not important. However, what is important is that we concur that art, in all its various forms, is in need of a Christian presence that is able to bring the truth of God to bear with utmost skill and mastery and to do it in solemn deference to the Crown Rights of King Jesus. It is to this end that every Christian artist must pray and work.

Bibliography

Delacroix, Eugène. Cited in Paul Signac, *D'Eugène Delacroix au Néo-Impressionisme.* Paris: Floury.

Kandinsky, Wassily. *Concerning the Spiritual in Art.* New York: Dover Publications, Inc., 1977.

"Religious Consciousness in Modern Art." Class notes. New Haven, CT: Yale University, 1982.

Rookmaaker, Hans. *Modern Art and the Death of Culture.* London: Inter-Varsity Press, 1970.

Schaeffer, Franky. *Addicted to Mediocrity: 20th Century Christians and the Arts.* Wheaton, IL: Crossway Books, 1981.

Schelling, Friedrich. Cited in Don Hudson, "On Earth As It Is In Heaven: Is Art Necessary for the Christian?" *Mars Hill Review,* no. 2 (May 1995): 31–40. http://www.leaderu.com/marshill/mhr02/don1.html.

Schilder, Klaas. *Christ and Culture.* Winnepeg, Manitoba: Premier Printing, 1977.

Sheesley, Joel C. "Content: The Substance of Things Hoped For." Keynote address, International Arts Movement, New York City, March 13, 1999.

Spaightwood Galleries, Upton, MA. "Emile Nolde (German, 1867–1956)," Online: http://spaightwoodgalleries.com/Pages/Nolde.html.

Wencelius, Leon G. "The Word of God and Culture" in *The Word of God and the Reformed Faith.* Grand Rapids: Eerdmans, 1942.